GORBACHEV

ANDREW LANGLEY

Heinemann Library
Chicago, Illinois

MW00799925

Customer Service 888-454-2279

Visit our website at www.heinemannlibrary.com

Originated by Dot Gradations, Ltd.
Printed by South China Printing Company, Ltd.

07 06 05 04 03
10 9 8 7 6 5 4 3 2 1

Library of Congress Cataloging-in-Publication Data
Langley, Andrew.
   Mikhail Gorbachev / Andrew Langley.
      p. cm. -- (Leading lives)
   Summary: Describes the life and political career of Mikhail Gorbachev and his legacy in the context of the demise of the Soviet Union and conditions in Russia today.
   Includes bibliographical references and index.
   ISBN 1-40340-831-9
   1. Gorbachev, Mikhail Sergeevich, 1931-   --Juvenile literature.
   2. Heads of state--Soviet Union--Biography--Juvenile literature.
   [1. Gorbachev, Mikhail Sergeevich, 1931-   . 2. Heads of state]
   I. Title. II. Series.
   DK290.3.G67L36 2003
   947.085'4'092--dc21
   [B]

2002012591

Acknowledgments
The author and publishers are grateful to the following for permission to reproduce copyright material: pp. 4, 21, 23, 26, 32, 48, 51 Popperfoto; pp. 5, 17, 35 Rex Features; pp. 6, 9, 11 Camera Press; pp. 15, 39–40, 42 Jim Zuckerman/Corbis; pp. 18, 27, 29 Hulton Archive; pp. 22, 30, 33, 36 Bettman/Corbis; pp. 24–25 Peter Newar's American Pictures; p. 44 Perfecto Romero/CSC; p. 52 Rolando Pujol/South American Pictures; p. 54 Popperfoto/Reuters.

Cover photograph of Mikhail Gorbachev reproduced with permission of Popperfoto.

Every effort has been made to contact copyright holders of any material reproduced in this book. Any omissions will be rectified in subsequent printings if notice is given to the publisher.

Some words are shown in bold, **like this.** You can find out what they mean by looking in the glossary.

Contents

The Coup

Mikhail Gorbachev, president of the **Soviet Union,** was on vacation. He had traveled with his wife, daughter, son-in-law, and grandchildren to their country home on the shore of the Black Sea. But he had little time to enjoy the view. On August 18, 1991, he was sitting at his desk hard at work.

Late in the afternoon, his chief guard entered. He told Gorbachev that some officials from Moscow wanted to see him. Gorbachev was not expecting visitors, and the interruption annoyed him. He reached for the telephone, and all five of the phone lines were dead. Now he was worried, and he told his family to expect trouble.

Taking over power

At last the chief guard showed the visitors in to see Gorbachev. An Emergency Committee of the **Communist** Party had sent the group of visitors. This committee was now in charge of the Soviet Union. They told Gorbachev they did not like his reform program and the changes it was making to the country. They feared that these changes were leading to

▼ Soviet tanks line up outside the **Kremlin** in Moscow immediately following the coup against Gorbachev in August 1991.

the breakup of the Soviet Union and the end of Communist Party power. Gorbachev must agree to restore the Party's control—or resign. The Communist Party had staged a **coup,** or attempt to remove Gorbachev from power by force.

Even though these people placed Gorbachev in a dangerous position, he refused to agree to either of these demands. He became a prisoner of his enemies. The next day military guards surrounded his country home, they cut off the telephone and television, and warships patrolled the shore. The only way the Gorbachevs could get news of the outside world was through a small portable radio.

Defeat of the plotters

Gorbachev could do little. The plotters had spread a story that the president was sick, and his wife Raisa worried that they might poison the family. She began to store food and, with her daughter, hid all the fruit in the house so that the grandchildren would not go hungry. Gorbachev tried to come up with a way out of this grim situation.

But the coup was already falling apart. Back in Moscow, the people had turned against the Emergency Committee. Huge crowds flocked to the White House, the Soviet Union's parliament building, to protect it from attack. Authorities arrested the conspirators, and the people broke the power of the Communist Party after 70 years of absolute rule. The liberation of the Soviet Union, begun by Mikhail Gorbachev, was about to take another giant step forward.

▶ *Gorbachev holds a press conference on his return to Moscow after the 1991 coup against him failed.*

Child of the Steppe

Mikhail Gorbachev was born on March 2, 1931, in the village of Privolnoye, in the Stavropol region of the southern Soviet Union. It was a remote spot, part of the vast rolling plain called the **steppe,** and it lay in the middle of some of the country's richest farmland. Gorbachev loved it.

FOR A MAP OF THE PLACES MENTIONED, SEE PAGE 9.

Gorbachev's parents were peasants, and they lived in a simple three-room dwelling built of mud and straw. His father was a quiet but intelligent man who ran the village's tractor factory. His mother was a much stronger character, and she had an important influence on young Gorbachev's life.

▲ *Part of the vast rolling grasslands of the steppe in the Stavropol region where Gorbachev grew up.*

FOR DETAILS ON KEY PEOPLE OF GORBACHEV'S TIME, SEE PAGE 58.

Fear and famine

Stavropol, with its fertile soil and warm summers, was a perfect area for growing crops and raising livestock. Yet when Gorbachev was a toddler, many people there were starving. This was because Joseph Stalin, the Soviet Union's leader at the time, wanted all peasants to join state-controlled **collective farms.** When a village such as Privolnoye refused to join, Stalin's men forcibly took away its food. During the winter of 1933–1934, one-third of Privolnoye's population starved to death. No wonder Gorbachev was a scrawny, underfed child.

Even a greater terror than famine existed, though. During the 1930s, Stalin's **secret police** arrested millions of people who he suspected of opposing his policies. He executed many of them or sent them to **labor camps.** In 1937, the government took Gorbachev's own grandfather away in the middle of the night. They released him a year later, but his tales of torture and imprisonment deeply shocked the young Gorbachev.

Nazi invasion

In 1941, during World War II (1939–1945), Gorbachev's father also left home, to fight with the Soviet army against the German **Nazis,** who had invaded the Soviet Union. The ten-year-old Gorbachev, as the only son, had to take on his father's role. Throughout the severe winter, he gathered fuel for the stove and fed the cow. Little time existed for school.

German troops swept into Privolnoye in August 1942. They took all the villagers' food supplies and threatened to execute all known **Communists.** This included the Gorbachevs, and so Gorbachev went into hiding in a nearby farmhouse. Early in 1943, Soviet troops liberated the region, but the Gorbachevs' troubles were far from over. Famine hit the village again, and Gorbachev's mother had no choice but to take her husband's clothes to market and swap them for food.

◀ *A German soldier strides past a burning ammunition dump during the 1941 German invasion of the Soviet Union.*

By the end of 1944, the Soviets had finally driven the Germans out of the **Soviet Union,** though the war did not end until 1945. Slowly, life returned to normal. Gorbachev went back to school, but after the horrors of wartime it seemed, he said, "a waste of time." His father came home from the army and resumed his job in the tractor factory. The family grew with the birth of a second son Alexander. By this time, however, Gorbachev was fifteen years old, and he never really became close to his much younger brother.

Work and high school

Gorbachev had worked on the **collective farm** during the war. By 1946 he was old enough to operate a large harvesting machine called a combine, cutting and gathering the wheat from the fields. It was grueling work. In dry weather he labored for up to twenty hours a day, with only three or four hours of sleep. The combine had no cab, so in cold weather he wrapped himself in straw to keep warm.

In 1948, Gorbachev began studying at the local high school. It was twelve miles

◀ Men and women plant crops on a collective farm near the Black Sea in 1937.

Collective farms and children

Beginning in 1928, the government took small farms away from individual peasants and combined these farms to form huge, state-controlled collective farms. The Soviets wanted to increase the production of food by using bigger fields and more machines. The Soviet government expected children such as Mikhail Gorbachev to help with this often backbreaking labor. In 1942, a new law required all boys and girls from the ages of 12 to 16 to work for at least 50 days each year on the farm.

(nineteen kilometers) away, and he had to walk there. As a result, he rented a room nearby during the week and returned home to his family on weekends.

Young Communist

Gorbachev studied hard and quickly became a star pupil, excelling in physics, chemistry, math, and history. At the same time, he took his first steps in politics and joined the Communist Party's youth organization, the **Komsomol.** Gorbachev was eager to find success in the wider world, far from Privolnoye. He could do this only as a party member.

▼ Gorbachev grew up in the Stavropol region of the Soviet Union and spent his early working life there.

Student in Moscow

Gorbachev left school with two awards. One was a silver medal for his school work. But he was always more proud of the other, the Order of the **Red Banner** of Labor, given for his heroic efforts on the combine. This award helped him greatly in his dream to leave the **steppe** of Stavropol. Most of his friends planned to attend local colleges, but Gorbachev wanted something better—a place at Moscow State University. With his Red Banner award, Moscow State soon accepted him.

Country boy in the capital

Gorbachev decided to study law, even though at the time he had only a vague idea of what the law was all about. The main reason, he wrote later, was that "the position of a judge or prosecutor impressed me." Clearly, the young man was interested in powerful roles.

After the endless plains of Stavropol, Moscow seemed to be an exciting place. Gorbachev went to

◀Gorbachev studied at Moscow State University from 1950 to 1955 and met his future wife Raisa there.

theaters and art galleries and visited Red Square, the **Kremlin** (the headquarters of the Soviet government), and other famous sites. But in the early months he felt ill at ease. He was obviously a peasant in the big city, proudly wearing his fur hat, his clumsy brown suit, and his Red Banner medal. At first, some fellow students mocked him, but they soon came to respect his intelligence and energy.

Life at the university was not luxurious. Gorbachev lived in a huge hostel (housing for students) outside the city. In his first year, the university squeezed him into a dormitory with 21 others. He had to make do with food sent from home and a shower in a public bathhouse twice a month.

Joining the party

Gorbachev became a full member of the **Communist** Party at age nineteen—the youngest possible age he could join. This act showed his immense ambitions. In the Soviet Union at that time, nobody could reach any position of authority without being a zealous and loyal party member. Gorbachev wanted power, and he knew that, even as a Communist, he would have to work hard to get it. He would also have to please the right people and never ask awkward questions.

FOR MORE ABOUT STALIN, SEE PAGE 58.

He learned this the hard way. In 1952, he complained that one of his teachers was not lecturing at all, but simply reading aloud page after page from a book by Stalin. The class reacted with shock and horror. No one was expected to criticize a teacher—let alone the great Stalin! The scandal went as far as the Moscow committee of the Communist Party, but eventually they pardoned Gorbachev, thanks to his worker and peasant background. He would be more careful in the future.

Even so, he found it hard to stay quiet when he saw injustice. In early 1953, a wave of anti-Jewish feeling spread through Moscow. Gorbachev was enraged to discover that a student mob had insulted and attacked one of his fellow students, a Jew. He leapt to his feet and fiercely defended his friend and that was the end of the attack.

Raisa

Gorbachev had already found another focus for his passionate nature—a beautiful fellow student named Raisa Titorenko. Small and elegant, Raisa was studying philosophy (she had earned a gold medal in school—one better than Gorbachev). He first met her in 1951. He tried hard to impress her though he admits, "I think I made a terrible fool of myself." But he kept trying, and soon they were spending all their free time together. By 1953 they had decided to get married, even though they were still poor students.

Somehow, Gorbachev had to raise enough money for them to set up a home. That summer, he returned to Privolnoye and worked hard as a mechanic at the tractor workshop. There was a good grain harvest that year, and Gorbachev and his father sold their crop for nearly 1,000 rubles (Soviet monetary unit)—a huge sum in those days. With his share, he was able to plan for the wedding.

Death of a dictator

At the same time, the Soviet population suffered a huge shock. Stalin died in March 1953. He had led the nation for 25 years. Even though millions had died during his rule, most Soviets had come to see him as an almost godlike figure. His death devastated Gorbachev, and he joined thousands of others as they filed past Stalin's coffin to view the body.

▲ *Joseph Stalin lies in state in Moscow in 1953. Gorbachev was among the huge crowds that filed past the body.*

Doubts began to surface in Gorbachev's mind as he stared at the body. "I searched for traces of his greatness, but there was something disturbing in his appearance which created mixed feelings," he wrote. Already, the people recognized that the Soviet state created by Stalin was unjust and doomed to fail. University friends described Gorbachev as a dissident — someone who disagreed with the political system. It was a dangerous position to take, but Gorbachev managed to keep his **liberal** views well hidden. On the surface, he was a devoted and energetic member of the Communist Party.

Gorbachev and Raisa were married in Moscow on September 25, 1953. They were still young students, and at first the authorities at the university would not let them live together. Each night, they had to go to their separate rooms. Gorbachev organized the student **Komsomol** in a protest against the rule. His efforts paid off, and eventually the university gave them a room to share. "I felt like a real family man," he wrote happily.

▲ *Mikhail Gorbachev and Raisa Titorenko were married in 1953.*

Shattered plans

But the happiness was short-lived. Gorbachev graduated from the university in 1955, and he confidently assumed that the government would give him a law job in Moscow. When he reported to the state **procurator's** (prosecutor's) office, however, they told him that there was no job for him. They thought law graduates were too young and innocent for the work involved.

This event was shattering. His grand career seemed to have ended before it began. His only option was to return to his home district and find work there. He would also need to find somewhere for Raisa and him to live. Leaving Raisa with her parents for a month, Gorbachev packed up their few belongings in two suitcases and a wooden crate. He then boarded the train back to Stavropol, where the **district prosecutor's** office soon hired him.

Now he had to find somewhere to live. He rented a tiny, shabby room, much of which was taken up by a stove and a long iron bed. They had no other furniture, so the crate came in handy as both a table and a bookcase. The bathroom was outside, and they had to collect water from a pump.

Change of direction

Raisa arrived there in 1956, and it was a bleak place for her. She was working and expecting a baby and had given up her postgraduate studies in Moscow to be with her husband. Worse still, Gorbachev suddenly decided to accept an entirely new job—one that would take him away from the family home for several nights each week.

Gorbachev hated his job as a lawyer. Even though Stalin was gone, his system of state control was still in place. This meant the politicians or Soviet **secret police,** called the **KGB,** controlled most law cases and had little to do with justice or fairness. To his great relief, Gorbachev's new post was with the local Komsomol in what the government called the Agitation and **Propaganda** Department.

His job was to spread the ideas of **Communism** among young people and encourage them to be model citizens. It meant traveling around the district, even to the most distant villages—sometimes by train or truck but often on foot.

Desolate villages

"As far as the eye could see, scattered at random, [were] low, smoke-belching huts . . . Down there, in those miserable dwellings, people led some kind of life. But the streets (if you could call them streets) were deserted. As if the plague had ravaged the entire village . . . And I told myself that this was the reason why the young fled from this godforsaken village. They fled from desolation and horror, from the terror of being buried alive . . . People deserve a better life—that was always on my mind."

(From Gorbachev's **memoir,** 1995, describing what he saw when he and some others visited a remote Stavropol village)

Political education

Gorbachev learned several important lessons from his time with the **Komsomol.** He saw for himself the desperate lives of those who lived in faraway areas. He noticed that many of the **Communist** Party bosses in the district were ignorant and greedy. Compared to other people, the party bosses looked well fed. "When you look at one of the local leaders, you see nothing outstanding apart from his belly," he told Raisa. Perhaps most important of all, he learned to be a public figure, making speeches and answering questions.

▼ This photo shows a typical Soviet village of the 1950s, with its shabby houses and muddy, unpaved roads.

◀ *Soviet leader Nikita Khrushchev waves to cheering crowds on a visit to Prague, which was the capital of Czechoslovakia, in 1957.*

Gorbachev's political views were given another jolt in the spring of 1956. The new Soviet leader, Nikita Khrushchev, made a speech attacking the character and leadership of Joseph Stalin. This shocked the entire country, for nobody had previously dared to suggest that Stalin had ever made mistakes. On his travels, people often asked Gorbachev to explain the meaning of Khrushchev's speech. Privately, he supported the leader's courageous step, which added to his own doubts about the Soviet government.

FOR DETAILS ON KEY PEOPLE OF GORBACHEV'S TIME, SEE PAGE 58.

Starting a family

The Gorbachevs' only daughter Irina was born in January 1957. However, the news that Raisa could never have another child clouded their joy. Life was difficult enough for her in any case. The lodgings were cold and cramped, and baby food was impossible to get. In addition, the family now had to live on one salary.

Things slowly got better. Raisa returned to work. She got a job at the local college, where she was paid more than her husband. Shortly after this, they rented a two-room apartment with a shared bathroom. Then, in 1958, party leaders elected Gorbachev as second secretary of the Stavropol Komsomol committee. His march to the top had begun.

Looking for Patrons

Gorbachev did not have long to wait for his next promotion. In March 1961 he became the **Komsomol's first secretary,** or leader for the whole district. This brought him an official car for traveling and a mountain of paperwork on his desk every day. This paperwork was mostly made up of orders from the **Central Committee.** It also took him to a higher level in the local political world. Now he was mixing with more powerful people.

Sideways and upward

That October, Gorbachev rubbed shoulders with the most powerful figures in the country. For the first time, he attended a **Party Congress** in Moscow as the Stavropol **delegate.** There he heard Khrushchev renew his attacks on Stalin and outline major reforms for the Soviet system. He admired Khrushchev's daring words but realized that the leader was probably making enemies who might eventually destroy him.

FOR A SUMMARY OF THE SOVIET SYSTEM OF GOVERNMENT, SEE PAGE 59.

Gorbachev knew that any politician, especially an ambitious peasant like himself, was bound to have enemies. What he needed were **patrons**—people in positions of power who could help and support him. Among the first of these was Fedor Kulakov, the party boss for the region, who quickly realized that Gorbachev was an outstanding and hardworking young man. Promotion soon followed. In 1962, the **Communist** Party transferred Gorbachev from the Komsomol to work directly for the Party.

His new job was to supervise the work of the regional Communist Party in three agricultural districts. Now he had to work even harder. "I spent days, and often nights, traveling around the district, visiting farms," he wrote. Less than a year later he took another big step up the ladder when Kulakov

▶ *Fedor Kulakov, a wily Communist Party official, helped launch Gorbachev's rise to the top.*

chose him to be head of the department that appointed party officials in the region. This was a responsible position and brought Gorbachev into almost daily contact with his boss.

The fall of Khrushchev

Kulakov was a valuable friend. He was highly ambitious and was hard at work climbing to the highest levels of the **Kremlin.** He was also cunning. When Khrushchev was in power, Kulakov agreed in public with everything Khrushchev said. But in private Kulakov plotted against the Soviet leader with others who feared that his reforms were going too far.

In October 1964 the Communists removed Khrushchev from power. They replaced him with Leonid Brezhnev, who was less interested in reforms. Kulakov immediately moved to Moscow, where he became secretary of agriculture. Now Gorbachev had a patron near the top. But he had also learned a valuable lesson from Khrushchev's fall. No leader could push through reforms if he had powerful enemies inside the party.

FOR DETAILS ON KEY PEOPLE OF GORBACHEV'S TIME, SEE PAGE 58.

With Kulakov's support, Gorbachev moved steadily higher. In 1966 he became **first secretary** of Stavropol city's party organization. This gave him more freedom to make his own decisions.

Learning from Raisa

Gorbachev was always proud of his wife's achievements. When she taught her college philosophy classes, he joined the course as a student. The pair would often hold debates about philosophical theories, and Raisa usually had the last word.

Raisa's views had a strong influence on her husband. To complete her doctor's degree at Moscow State University in 1967, she had studied the way the government ran **collective farms.** She found that farmers who were allowed to make their own decisions about growing and selling their crops produced better crops than those who stayed under strict state control. Gorbachev learned a lot from her work.

Standing still under Brezhnev

In August 1968, the government called Gorbachev to Moscow, where they told him that he

◀ *Czech leader Alexander Dubcek (far right) greets Brezhnev (center) during an apparently friendly meeting in Bratislava in 1968. Soviet tanks arrived two weeks later to prevent Dubcek from carrying out his liberal policies.*

was now second-in-command of party affairs in Stavropol. But he had hardly settled into this post before news came of the invasion of Czechoslovakia by armed forces of the **Warsaw Pact,** a group of Eastern European **Communist** countries.

The brutal treatment of the Czechs saddened Gorbachev. At home, too, there was a renewed clampdown on anyone who questioned the Communist Party line or suggested reforms.

Keeping down the Czechs

The Communist Party had governed Czechoslovakia since 1948. This meant that it was under Soviet rule as part of the **Eastern bloc.** Alexander Dubcek became party leader in 1968 and introduced many **liberal** reforms, such as freedom of the press and contact with noncommunist countries. He promised **"socialism** with a human face." The **Kremlin** met his statements with anger and alarm. Brezhnev and other Soviet leaders believed that Dubcek's measures would weaken Communist control in Czechoslovakia. They feared that calls for reform might spread to neighboring Soviet-controlled Communist countries. So, in August 1968, more than 200,000 Soviet troops, backed by small forces from other Warsaw Pact armies, invaded Czechoslovakia. The Soviets arrested and imprisoned Dubcek and installed hard-line Communist officials in his place. The country became an obedient Communist state once again.

◀ A lone protester tries to stop Soviet tanks as they grind through the streets of Bratislava during the Soviet invasion of Czechoslovakia in 1968.

Party Boss

In the spring of 1970, the party leaders elected Gorbachev **first secretary** for the whole Stavropol territory. This was a position of real power at last. The first secretary controlled the entire management system of the region. No one could make appointments without his approval. Even more important, first secretaries made up the majority of the party's **Central Committee** for the country (which Gorbachev joined in 1971). Their votes were important in deciding government actions.

The outside world

Gorbachev's new post also brought him a precious privilege—he could make visits to **Western** Europe. Since 1966, he and Raisa had traveled to countries in **Communist** Eastern Europe, including East Germany, Bulgaria, and Czechoslovakia. But these governments ran their countries on strict Soviet lines, with state-controlled farming and industry and no freedom of speech. Gorbachev, for example, was depressed to find **East Berlin** a "cold and forbidding" place.

The Cold War

During World War II (1939–1945), the United States and the Soviet Union fought on the same side. After the war ended in 1945, the two countries became enemies. The Soviet Union wanted to help spread Communism to other countries. The capitalist United States wanted to prevent this. The two sides never fought each other in battle, so the hostility between the two powers never became "hot." Instead, in 1947 a U.S. politician described the situation as a "cold war." The term caught on and became the name for the long period of tension that existed between capitalist and Communist countries between 1945 and 1991.

Now he could travel through the **iron curtain** to the **capitalist** West—something the Soviets allowed few people to do. In 1972, he and Raisa visited Belgium and the Netherlands. Trips to Italy, France, and West Germany followed during the 1970s.

What Gorbachev saw astounded him. The Communist Party so tightly controlled the Soviet news media that little information about the West ever reached ordinary people in the **Soviet Union.** As a result, many Soviets were ignorant and mistrustful of the West. Suddenly, he discovered that people in Western Europe could be open and honest in their opinions about anything, including their governments. Even more shocking was the fact that their wealth and living conditions were much higher than those of people at home. How could a capitalist society work so much better than a **socialist** one?

Living standards

"The question haunted me: why was the standard of living in our country lower than in other developed countries? It seemed that our aged leaders were not especially worried about our lower living standards, our unsatisfactory way of life, and our falling behind in the field of advanced technologies."

(From Gorbachev's **memoir,** 1995)

New patrons

By the mid-1970s, Gorbachev had found two new and powerful allies. One was Mikhail Suslov, a cunning and sinister politician who had worked for both Stalin and Khrushchev. The other was Yuri Andropov, head of the Soviet Union's dreaded **secret police,** the **KGB.** Andropov was an intelligent, honest man who secretly hated the corrupt and stifling atmosphere of Brezhnev's leadership. He soon realized that he could trust Gorbachev, for he was a man who looked to a better future.

FOR DETAILS ON KEY PEOPLE OF GORBACHEV'S TIME, SEE PAGE 58.

Agricultural change

Gorbachev had to prove himself. As **first secretary,** he was in a position of real authority. Now he had to show that he could make big decisions and put major plans into effect. Stavropol, a key farming region, badly needed improvements to make its harvests bigger and its farming methods more efficient. It was the perfect place for him to make a name for himself.

Gorbachev began by tackling the crop failures caused by drought. Back in Stalin's time, people took the first steps by building a canal that would bring precious water to the dry, windswept area. But the project had crawled along, and workers had still not completed it. Gorbachev flung all his enormous energy into the project. He wrote action plans, pestered ministers, and even sent his plans to Brezhnev himself. The result was spectacular. By 1978, workers had finished the Stavropol Canal.

There were other big problems to solve. How much grain should farmers grow? Was there enough food for the cattle and pigs to last through the winter? How could farmers quickly increase the output of meat? Gorbachev found solutions to all these questions, often by challenging the central government.

Even so, he could not win every battle. Thanks partly to Raisa's research into **collective farming,** Gorbachev had encouraged independent farmers. He allowed small groups to farm plots of land in whatever way they wanted. His ideas were a spectacular success, and harvests on these plots improved by 600 percent. But in 1977 Kulakov, the agriculture secretary in Moscow, decreed that a new system had to be put in place. Huge teams of laborers now harvested the crops, marching across the country like an army. This policy forced Gorbachev to give up his experiment.

Farewell to the steppe

Gorbachev's achievements in Stavropol marked him as an up-and-coming politician. His first **patron** Kulakov died in 1978, but he still had the powerful support of Suslov and Andropov. He also grew closer to the prime minister, Aleksei Kosygin, and the pair would go for long walks together in the hills near the Black Sea.

The death of Kulakov left a vacancy in the **Politburo**—the highest circle of **Communist** power, where party leaders made important decisions. Who would fill it? To his surprise, party leaders named Gorbachev the new secretary of agriculture, thanks to the influence of Andropov and the grudging approval of Brezhnev. With one leap, he was inside the **Kremlin,** the center of Soviet government.

He and Raisa were sad to leave the peace and natural beauty of Stavropol, where they had lived so long and raised their daughter Irina. Now the whole Gorbachev family had to make themselves a new home in faraway Moscow.

▼ *This photo shows the highly decorated outside of the Grand Kremlin Palace in Moscow, the main center of Soviet government. Gorbachev returned to Moscow in 1978 as secretary of agriculture.*

In the Politburo

To Gorbachev, Moscow seemed like a strange and unfriendly place, and it took the family some weeks to find a place to live. "To begin with," wrote Gorbachev, "we felt lonely." Many people in the **Central Committee** looked on him as just a country bumpkin from the provinces. But he plunged straight into work. Eventually the family, including Irina and her new husband Anatoly, moved into a comfortable apartment and were given a country home on the river near the city.

A shrinking economy

Gorbachev soon made an impact in the highest levels of government. He worked in his office for up to fifteen hours a day. He buzzed around the **Kremlin,** asking questions, singing, and cracking jokes, but he was always eager to learn and understand what was going on. His energy and enthusiasm led one dazed colleague to exclaim, "He's an insatiable hurricane of a person." By this, he meant that Gorbachev was never satisfied and moved on with great power from one challenge to another.

But the more Gorbachev learned, the more uneasy he grew. The **Soviet Union's** economy was falling apart. State-run factories and farms were so badly organized that hundreds of thousands of laborers never bothered to go to work. Most products, such as tractors and cars, were of poor quality. The economy of the countryside was in tatters, because the **collective farming** system could not repay huge government loans. Poor farming practices damaged the farmland. Worst of all, the government wasted 25 percent of its money on producing weapons, as it tried to keep up with the United States in the **arms race.** Brezhnev and the other aging leaders closed their eyes to the growing difficulties.

Mounting crisis

As secretary of agriculture, Gorbachev had big problems.
The 1979 harvest was poor, and he knew that there was going
to be a shortage of food. He proposed **liberal** changes to the
collective farming system to encourage better harvests.
He also suggested that the country should buy badly needed
extra grain from the United States.

The arms race

Since the 1960s, the military competition between the United States and
the **Soviet Union** had sped up. Each country spent huge sums of money
to build all kinds of weapons, especially **nuclear weapons,** in a race to
gain superiority. By 1980, the two sides had 40,000 nuclear warheads
between them—enough to destroy all life on Earth several times over.

In the late 1970s, the two sides tried to agree on ways of avoiding this
terrible threat. They signed a **Strategic Arms** Limitation Treaty (SALT)
in 1979 to limit the number of nuclear weapons produced. A year later,
the United States withdrew from the treaty to protest the Soviet invasion
of Afghanistan.

The invasion of Afghanistan

On Christmas Day 1979, Soviet tanks and troops invaded
Afghanistan to help strengthen the **socialist** government there.
The conflict was a complete disaster. The huge Soviet army, with
all its modern weapons, could not defeat the poorly armed
Islamic resistance fighters. Worse still, the invasion angered
the rest of the world. In protest, the United States broke off
trade agreements and refused to sell any of its grain to the
Soviet Union.

▲ *Soviet tanks arrive in Afghanistan in 1979 at the start of the ill-fated invasion.*

Suddenly, agriculture became a hot topic. Gorbachev now had a chance to draw up bold plans to improve the country's farming and avoid the need to buy food from other countries. He worked hard, studying reports, consulting experts, and battling to get his ideas accepted. In the end his food program, introduced in 1982, was a costly failure—largely because dishonest officials used it for their own purposes.

The Politburo's old men

The Afghan War was yet another disaster for Soviet leaders. By this time, the government had reached a standstill, and no one was prepared to make tough decisions. The meetings of the **Politburo** became almost a joke. The average age of its members was over 70. Brezhnev was sick and sometimes showed up drunk, and few on the committee could hear what he said. Andropov and other senior members were interested only in taking his place as soon as he died.

Gorbachev also discovered that work got in the way of his social life. He had little time for his family or for rest. The Politburo did not encourage meeting colleagues outside the office or visiting their homes. Politburo members were afraid that Brezhnev might hear about such meetings and think that people were plotting against him in private.

Raisa found it difficult to get used to the limited kind of life led by the "Kremlin wives." She thought they were dull and stuck-up, and she made all her friends outside the tight government circle. She went back to college and began to study English. With Gorbachev, she enjoyed exploring the historic parts of Moscow and attending plays, operas, and concerts—something few other Politburo couples would have done.

Death of Brezhnev

The old center of Soviet power began to break up when Mikhail Suslov died in January 1982. Andropov seized his place as deputy leader—he made sure of it by grabbing his chair at a Politburo session! By now Brezhnev, who was sick, could not hold a pen or speak in public. Although the Politburo kept his health a secret from the Soviet people, an emergency medical team surrounded Brezhnev. He died in November. Could this be the end of the long period of **stagnation?**

Life under Andropov

Andropov, the new **general secretary** of the Soviet Union, was one of Gorbachev's best political friends. This meant promotion and much more responsibility. Gorbachev took over Andropov's position as second-in-command of the party, and the Politburo put him in charge of the country's economy. Among the perks of his new job was a visit to Canada, where he impressed everyone with his intelligence and sense of humor.

FOR DETAILS ON KEY PEOPLE OF GORBACHEV'S TIME, SEE PAGE 58.

Andropov at last had the chance to introduce reforms in the Soviet Union and to forge a warmer relationship with the United States. He began energetically with campaigns against dishonest officials, poor work performance, and excessive drinking. He opened talks with the U.S. president Ronald Reagan on reducing the numbers of nuclear missiles in Europe.

But these projects never succeeded. Andropov, like Brezhnev, was old and sick. Rumors began to spread that he would not last long. When he died, in February 1984, members of the **Politburo** were still afraid to look to the future. Gorbachev was the obvious choice as new leader, but most thought that at age 53 he was too young. So they elected Konstantin Chernenko instead, who was 73 years old and dying from asthma and other diseases. For the

◀ *Gorbachev (front row, second from right) stands with other Soviet leaders to pay his last respects to Yuri Andropov in 1984.*

◀ *Prime Minister Margaret Thatcher and her husband Denis greet the Gorbachevs on their first visit to Great Britain in 1984.*

third time, the Soviet people had a leader who was elderly, feeble, and out of touch.

Last of the old men

Now Gorbachev was clearly next in line for the leadership, but he had to be patient. Fortunately, he had plenty to do. With Chernenko too sick to travel, Gorbachev became the country's representative. In June 1984, he led the party delegation to Italy to attend the funeral of the Italian Communist leader Enrico Berlinguer.

A few months later, he and Raisa made their first visit to Great Britain, where they met British prime minister Margaret Thatcher. The trip was a huge success. The British public was amazed to find that Raisa was glamorous and lively—nothing like other Soviet wives they had seen. And Thatcher quickly warmed to Gorbachev's charm and energy. "I like Mr. Gorbachev," she said. "We can do business together."

Some of the older **Kremlin** leaders were envious of Gorbachev's popularity at home and abroad. But they were too late to stop his rise to power, for he had great support from regional officials. As Chernenko became sicker, Gorbachev started taking the chair at weekly Politburo meetings. When the old general secretary died in March 1985, the members had no choice but to propose that Mikhail Gorbachev should take his place.

Soviet Leader

On March 10, 1985, the **Central Committee** of the Soviet **Communist** Party elected Mikhail Gorbachev as their new **general secretary.** He responded with a speech setting out his aims. He said that the **Soviet Union** had to move forward by developing its science and technology and by making its society more **democratic.** The party and the state would operate with greater openness. He declared that he wanted to stop the **arms race** with the **West** and to reduce the number of **nuclear weapons.**

FOR A SUMMARY OF THE SOVIET SYSTEM OF GOVERNMENT, SEE PAGE 59.

Building a power base

Many general secretaries had spoken this way in the past. Few Soviets expected that this stocky peasant from Stavropol would keep his promises any better than previous leaders. But Gorbachev was not only determined to make major changes to the Soviet system, he was also cunning enough to push the

▼ *Gorbachev's only child Irina (left) with her daughter, Kseniya, and husband Anatoly at a Red Square military parade in 1985.*

changes through. He knew that the **Politburo** had to approve all new measures, and he could not work without its support.

His first task was to shuffle the members of the Politburo so that most of them were on his side. He got rid of the old guard from the Brezhnev era, including the long-time foreign minister Andrei Gromyko (known in the West as "Grim Grom" because of his negative attitude). Then Gorbachev gave powerful posts to younger, more **liberal** officials.

Outside the Politburo he made even more changes. He fired half of the department heads, in addition to 39 out of 101 Soviet ministers. Throughout the Soviet Union, he replaced about twenty percent of all officials. Reform was in the air as Gorbachev stamped his authority on the government from the beginning.

Meeting the people

Next, he did something even more extraordinary. He started making regular visits to factories and towns, mingling with people and talking to them. Raisa often went with him. Gorbachev wanted to hear what ordinary Soviets had to say, and he scolded local officials who tried to silence them when he was present. No Soviet leader had ever acted so openly and freely before.

As Soviet leader, Gorbachev had little free time to pursue other interests. When time was available, he liked to visit the theater and art galleries with Raisa. Finding some time to enjoy the peace of the countryside was also important to him.

◀ *U.S. president Ronald Reagan and Gorbachev share a joke during their first summit meeting in 1985.*

SDI and summits

The Soviet economy of 1985 was in poor shape. Gorbachev knew that one of the major causes was the huge amount of money the government spent on defense. Every year, huge sums went toward building weapons and maintaining the armed forces. Even so, the Soviet Union was falling behind the United States, which had suddenly increased its buildup of arms. Most worrisome of all was the **Strategic Defense Initiative (SDI)**—a U.S. idea to install an outer-space defense system that could destroy enemy missiles with laser beams.

Gorbachev had to start new talks on stopping the **arms race.** He arranged a **summit** meeting with U.S. president Ronald Reagan in Geneva, Switzerland, for November 1985. For the first time in many years, the heads of the **capitalist** and **Communist** worlds met in a warm and constructive way. After three days, they signed a joint statement that said "Nuclear war cannot be won and must never be fought." They promised to improve relations between the two countries.

Retreat from Afghanistan

Gorbachev and Reagan held their second summit meeting in 1986 in Reykjavik, Iceland. Once again, they edged closer to agreement on reducing arms and even getting rid of nuclear weapons. But they did not sign a treaty, and the **superpowers** remained suspicious of each other.

Chernobyl

The Soviet authorities had always told everyone that the nuclear power plant at Chernobyl, in Ukraine, was perfectly safe. Then on April 26, 1986, one of the reactors blew up, killing 31 people and injuring more than 500 others. The blast spread a cloud of dangerous **radioactive dust** over large parts of Europe, and crops grown in these areas had high levels of radiation. Fortunately, this effect wore off quickly. Near Chernobyl, however, radiation levels had long-term effects. In the next five years, thousands of people in the Chernobyl area died of **leukemia** and other illnesses.

The United States knew that the Soviet Union was still in a terrible mess. The United States did not think they could be trusted. These fears increased in mid-1986 after a massive explosion at a **nuclear power plant** at Chernobyl. If a tragic accident like that could happen, how could the Soviets control their nuclear weapons?

Gorbachev was sincere in wanting to end the **Cold War**—and other wars. The most obvious war was in Afghanistan. Despite many casualties, the Soviets had no success. In November 1986, he withdrew 6,000 troops. This still left more than 90,000 troops there. But that act started the Soviet retreat from the disastrous war.

▲ *This photo shows the ruins of the fourth block of the Chernobyl nuclear power plant.*

9

Glasnost and Perestroika

By early 1987, Gorbachev had good reason to be hopeful. Abroad, he found a new ally in his search for peace and stability. The British prime minister Margaret Thatcher visited Moscow. Although strongly anti-Communist, she liked Gorbachev's energetic and aggressive style, which was similar to her own. Once again, the two enjoyed a warm, honest discussion, sometimes shouting, sometimes laughing. From then on, Thatcher worked hard to improve the relationship between Gorbachev and Reagan, helping to smooth out differences and misunderstandings between them.

Rebuilding the Soviet Union

At home, Gorbachev believed that two new policies—**glasnost** and **perestroika**—would turn the **Soviet Union** away from the decay, corruption, and nightmares of its past. *Glasnost* means "openness," and for the first time in Soviet history the Soviet government encouraged people to talk

▼ *Gorbachev made many trips around the country to meet the Soviet people. Here, he talks to factory workers near Moscow in 1987.*

honestly about their government and to make criticisms. The Soviet government allowed foreign radio stations, such as Great Britain's BBC and the U.S. Voice of America, to broadcast in the Soviet Union. Books once banned as anti-Communist were published at last. By mid-1987, the government had set free more than 300 **political prisoners**.

Perestroika means "rebuilding." Gorbachev was determined to transform the country's economy and industry into something that worked in a modern, open way. This included what was called "the human factor"—taking more notice of what ordinary workers wanted and how they were treated. The government was going to invest more money into factories and into the creation of new industries.

The backlash

But this more **liberal** rule brought its own problems. Soviets now felt bold enough to criticize Gorbachev himself. Many strict **Communists** hated the way that Gorbachev's policies had taken much of the party's power away. Also, ordinary people found that the rebuilding of the economy did not necessarily mean that working and living conditions improved. Gorbachev was angry with the complainers who wanted, he said, "to improve things without changing anything."

One of Gorbachev's strongest critics was Boris Yeltsin, a rough, tough member of the **Politburo.** In October 1987, he caused a sensation by claiming that perestroika was moving too slowly, that Gorbachev's promises were empty, and that fellow party members were bullies. Gorbachev was furious. A few days later he forced Yeltsin to resign, saying "I will never allow you back into big-time politics." Little did he know that he had made a powerful enemy.

FOR DETAILS ON KEY PEOPLE OF GORBACHEV'S TIME, SEE PAGE 58.

▲ *Still smiling, Gorbachev and Reagan sign a historic arms agreement treaty in December 1987 that banned medium-range nuclear missiles.*

Summit success

In December, Gorbachev went to the United States to meet President Reagan for a third **summit** conference in Washington, D.C. This was a crucial meeting, a last chance to agree on ways to end the long **Cold War.** Once again, the pair got along well, and the two sides drew up a treaty that swept away hundreds of nuclear missiles from Europe.
The signing of the treaty was a significant worldwide event. Broadcasting companies showed it live on television in both the United States and the Soviet Union.

The American public loved the Gorbachevs. A wave of "Gorbymania" spread through Washington as the couple toured the streets, talking and shaking hands. *Time* magazine named Gorbachev its "Person of the Year" for his part in promoting world peace. At a farewell dinner, he gave an emotional speech, saying "What we have achieved is . . . a revival of hope."

Six months later, Reagan and Gorbachev built on their achievements at a fourth summit. This time it was held in Moscow. They made some progress in agreeing to get rid of more **nuclear weapons,** but the biggest success was in opening up the Soviet Union to the outside world. Reagan became the first U.S. president to talk to ordinary Soviet citizens. He also made a speech to Moscow students and met critics of the government. The Communist Party never would have allowed it to happen before Gorbachev became leader.

A new kind of government

Gorbachev had yet more surprises up his sleeve. At the party conference in June 1988, he proposed that the country should be run in the future by a single president and a **Congress of People's Deputies.** People would choose the leaders in free elections. Until this point, the **Communist** Party had been the only political party allowed. Communists, therefore, held all the most important positions of power, and the party strictly controlled all elections. Now, there could be open competition. It spelled the end of the **one-party** system.

The government pushed the modernizing program ahead at a party meeting in September. Several elderly party leaders retired, including Andrei Gromyko, who had held the title of president, though he had no real power. Who would take his place? The answer was Gorbachev, who was quickly elected to the post. He was now both the Communist Party's **general secretary** and the Soviet Union's head of state.

10

The Iron Curtain Disappears

On December 7, 1988, Gorbachev rose to make one of the most important speeches of his life. He was at the **United Nations** headquarters in New York City, delivering a speech to representatives from more than 150 countries.

Soviet leaders before him would have spoken of the class struggle, of great **Communist** achievements, and of U.S. aggression. Gorbachev was entirely different. He declared an end to the **Cold War,** an end to his country's isolation from the **Western** world, and the beginning of people's freedom to choose for themselves. He topped this by announcing that he would cut the size of the Soviet army by half a million troops.

He stunned his audience—and then they gave him a standing ovation. He became a hero throughout the United States. Crowds chanted "Gorby! Gorby!" wherever he appeared.

▼ *Gorbachev makes his stirring speech to the United Nations General Assembly in 1988, promising a major cut in Soviet armed forces.*

The gathering storm

Back home, it was a different matter. Gorbachev's policy of free choice horrified traditional Communists. They wondered what that would mean to the countries of the **Eastern bloc.** The Soviet Union had controlled these neighboring countries for 40 years. Now they could choose to go their own way. In addition, the **Soviet Union,** which consisted of fifteen separate **republics,** was in danger of splitting up.

Events soon confirmed their fears. In January 1989, Estonia, one of the Soviet republics, made the first attempt of acting for itself. The Estonian government passed a new law that required all residents to be able to speak the Estonian language. Other republics quickly adopted the same laws for their own languages. It was a small step on the road to independence from Moscow, but it was a significant one.

FOR A MAP OF THE PLACES MENTIONED, SEE PAGE 52.

Soviet troops had always been there to back up unpopular Communist governments in Eastern Europe. Now the Soviets were bringing them home. People felt free to air their views. In Hungary, the parliament passed **liberal** new laws. Hungarian soldiers began cutting down the wire fences that lined their border with Austria. Protests and demonstrations broke out in Czechoslovakia as well as in the Soviet republics of Azerbaijan and Georgia.

The Eastern bloc

"An **iron curtain** has descended across the continent," said British prime minister Winston Churchill in 1946. He meant that Europe was split between the Communist East and the **capitalist West.** The Western countries were largely free and independent. The Soviet Union tightly controlled those in the East, which were organized Communist governments. The Berlin Wall symbolized the division of the continent. The Communists built it across the middle of the city of Berlin in 1961 to prevent people from fleeing to the West.

Rejecting Communism

As Gorbachev had promised, in March 1989 the Soviet people voted in the first free election they had ever known. They were electing their first **democratic** parliament for the **Soviet Union Congress of People's Deputies.** The result of the election was a bitter blow for the **Communist** Party. Even though the majority of members won their seats, a large minority (twenty percent) lost theirs. Communists never believed that they could ever fail in an election.

Outsiders and independent candidates triumphed as they defeated many powerful members of the Communist Party. One of those who shot back to power was Boris Yeltsin. Five million people voted him in as mayor of Moscow. As expected, the ruling Congress Committee elected Gorbachev as president, but Yeltsin's return must have been a troubling sign. It showed that people wanted to see faster change and were prepared to support politicians who promised this.

The fall of the Berlin Wall

Outside the Soviet Union, events were happening with bewildering speed. Communist Eastern Europe, which had once seemed as solid as a rock, fell to pieces as Soviet control over the region disappeared. In June 1989, the people of Poland removed the Communist Party from power in a free election. The Hungarian government opened its borders to allow people to flee through the country from East Germany to the West.

Gorbachev made it clear that he would not interfere with this process. In October, he visited **East Berlin,** the capital city divided by a concrete wall. Hordes of demonstrators met him, shouting **"Perestroika!** Gorbachev! Help us!" and "We need freedom!" The demonstrators had been demanding democratic reforms in East Germany and investigation of political wrongdoing.

East Berlin was now the focus of the freedom movement. The protests grew bigger and louder. On November 9, people forced the government to open its borders to the **West.** Over half a million people gathered on both sides of the wall and attacked the concrete with chisels and crowbars. All over the world, television viewers watched in amazement as Germans destroyed this symbol of the **Cold War.**

▼ *Ecstatic crowds pour through an opening in the Berlin Wall in November 1989. This event marked the beginning of the end of Soviet control in Eastern Europe.*

The amazing transformation galloped forward. In Bulgaria, a reform group took over the national **Politburo.** In Czechoslovakia, voters swept the **Communist** Party from office and replaced them with reformers. Among the leaders was Alexander Dubcek, who had led the **liberal** movement back in 1968. In December the people of Romania, who had suffered years of poverty and lack of freedom, staged a **coup** to bring down the hated Communist **dictator** Nikolai Ceaucescu. Authorities executed him by firing squad. By early 1990, the Communist empire in Eastern Europe had vanished.

FOR A MAP OF THE PLACES MENTIONED, SEE PAGE 52.

Trouble on the doorstep

The year 1989 had been a triumphant one for Gorbachev. With his enormous energy and idealism, he had driven through reforms that had changed the face of the world. The **Cold War** was coming to an end. He had given the people free elections and encouraged liberal governments in the **Eastern bloc**. On trips abroad people treated him as a hero. At the end of the year, he met the pope in Rome and held an important **summit** meeting with the new U.S. president George H. W. Bush.

But Gorbachev had made one major error. He believed that he could control the speed and spread of change, but it was soon like a runaway train. This was especially clear back home in the Soviet Union. For a start, the economy was in ruins. His policy of **perestroika** may have gotten rid of the stifling state control of industry, but it also exposed the fact that the country was running at a massive loss. Prices soared, standards of living fell, and many people found themselves out of work.

Gorbachev's policy of **glasnost** gave people the freedom to criticize their government. But it also meant that he faced growing opposition from two sides. Old-fashioned party members thought that he was betraying the ideals of the 1917 **Russian Revolution** and abandoning the strict Communist code. Ordinary workers, on the other hand, wanted much more freedom and an end to the party's hold on power. They began to go on **strike** for higher wages and for a bigger say in how their companies were managed.

Rebellious republics

Then there was the future of the **Soviet Union** itself. Gorbachev had encouraged the Communist countries of Eastern Europe to become independent of Moscow, so it was not surprising that the individual Soviet republics demanded liberty as well. This, for Gorbachev, was going too far. Releasing the fifteen republics to govern themselves would destroy the Soviet Union. It could not be allowed to happen.

However, the republics were utterly determined to break away, even if this brought bloodshed. In April 1989, Soviet troops using poison gas and truncheons (short, thick sticks that police officers use as weapons) broke up a massive demonstration in Tbilisi, the capital city of Georgia. Nineteen Georgians died. In January 1990, Gorbachev traveled to Lithuania to try to convince the people that their country should remain part of the Soviet Union. But the Lithuanians ignored his speeches. In March they declared their independence and elected their own president. Gorbachev's worst nightmare was coming true.

11

End of an Empire

FOR A MAP
OF THE
PLACES
MENTIONED,
SEE PAGE 52.

The situation grew steadily worse throughout 1990. After Lithuania's defiance, more **republics** announced that they were breaking away from the **Soviet Union**—Estonia in March, Latvia in May, and Ukraine in July. Belarus, Turkmenistan, Tajikistan, and others followed them. Gorbachev tried harsh methods to keep control. He cut off oil supplies to Lithuania and sent troops to impose order in the capital city of Vilnius. But nothing could stop the rush toward independence.

▲ *On the streets of Vilnius, a woman gives out soup to demonstrators protesting the Soviet crackdown in Lithuania.*

The party's over

Gorbachev was now in an impossible position. One side thought he was changing things too fast, and the other thought he was not changing them fast enough. The argument about the **Communist** Party illustrates this situation most clearly. At a **Central Committee** meeting in February, Gorbachev proposed that there should be more than one political party in the Soviet Union. The Communist Party must give up its leading role. This caused a stormy debate, but the Central Committee accepted the proposals.

In March 1990, the **Congress of People's Deputies** elected Gorbachev president of the Soviet Union and gave him more wide-ranging powers to govern. He was still a loyal member of the Communist Party, and it seemed that he was in a strong position. But, in fact, he was getting left behind by the speed of change.

A parallel president

Gorbachev found that his popularity was plummeting. He had given people more freedom, but he could not provide jobs, opportunities, or hope for the future. Pitiful shortages existed in stores, and people even found bread hard to find. At the annual Moscow May Day parade, which honored working people, the angry crowd greeted him with jeers and roars of "Resign!"

The next blow fell a few weeks later, when the Congress of People's Deputies in **Russia** elected a new chairman. They rejected the official Communist candidate. Instead, they chose a man who had resigned from the Communist Party and the **Politburo,** defied Gorbachev, and won enormous support— Boris Yeltsin.

"We haven't just seized an office," said Yeltsin. "We have seized the whole of Russia!" He was right. Gorbachev might be the leader of the Soviet Union as a whole, but Yeltsin was leader of by far the biggest and most important part of it. Russia controlled much of the Soviet Union's trade and industry and was the center of finance and government. Within two weeks, Yeltsin announced that Russia was a **sovereign state**—which meant that it, too, had declared its independence from the Soviet Union.

The crisis grows

Once again, Gorbachev found he had more friends and supporters abroad than at home. In October 1990, he was given the **Nobel Prize** for peace, one of the most important international awards. In November, a protester fired shots at

him during a parade in Moscow (luckily he was not hurt). Two weeks later, he signed an important treaty to limit troop numbers in Europe. In December foreign minister Eduard Shevardnadze, once one of Gorbachev's closest allies, resigned from his post, warning of the danger of **dictatorship** in the **Soviet Union.**

The year 1991 began grimly in the Baltic republics, which were still making angry demands for independence.

◀ *Gorbachev receives the Nobel Prize for peace in October 1990. While many in the **Western** world welcomed his reforms, others within the Communist Party felt that Gorbachev's policies might result in the breakup of the Soviet Union.*

Bloodstained hands

"The president will soon be surrounded by colonels and generals. Gorbachev is the only leader in Soviet history who has not stained his hands with blood, and we would like to remember him for that. But a moment will come when they will instigate a bloodbath, and later they will wipe their bloodstained hands against your suit, and you will be to blame for everything."

(From a speech by Soviet filmmaker, Ales Adamovich, warning Gorbachev of the tragedy that would follow should he use force to halt the breakup of the Soviet Union)

◀ *Moldovans rejoice in 1991, after their parliament declared its independence from Soviet control.*

Gorbachev ordered paratroopers to seize public buildings in Vilnius. Violence killed thirteen Lithuanians, and five protesters died in clashes with Soviet soldiers in Riga, the Latvian capital. Too late, Gorbachev realized he was making a terrible mistake and withdrew the troops—but many people already saw him as a hard-line bully. Georgia declared its independence from the Soviet Union in April.

Losing control

Meanwhile, Boris Yeltsin was building support as Russia's leader. He signed an agreement with the Baltic states, promising to give military help when needed against outside attacks. In June he won the country's first **democratic** election to choose an official president of **Russia.** Now, two rival bosses were ruling much the same territory. Yeltsin, however, was in a much stronger position than Gorbachev.

Gorbachev tried hard to avoid disaster and regain the people's respect. He signed a new treaty with the United States, which cut the number of nuclear missiles on both sides. He tried— unsuccessfully—to get a huge loan from the United States to help the Soviet economy. Finally, he drew up a new plan for the union, which he called the Nine-Plus-One Agreement. This would do away with the old **Soviet Union** and replace it with a looser Union of Sovereign States, made up of nine republics plus Russia. In need of a break, he flew off with his family for a vacation at their country home near the Black Sea.

49

Bowing Out

Time had run out for Mikhail Gorbachev. The rise of the anti-Communist Yeltsin, the coming shakeup of the **Soviet Union,** the disappearance of the Soviet Empire in Europe, the end of **Communist** Party supremacy, the unrest in the streets of Moscow—all of these events horrified the old guard of the **Kremlin.** Now, they were taking action. While the Gorbachevs were safely out of the way, a group of senior Communist Party officials hatched their plot to seize power. Among the members of this emergency committee were the Soviet vice president, the head of the **KGB,** the prime minister, and the defense minister.

The collapse of the coup

"I would not say that my holiday that year was a real rest," wrote Gorbachev later. He was put under house arrest by the emergency committee. Raisa was, as always, a tower of strength. After four days of fear and uncertainty, the plot collapsed. The danger suddenly disappeared, and the Gorbachevs were free to return to Moscow.

Why did the **coup** fail? To begin with, the members of the emergency committee had no real plan. Even when they appeared on television to announce the takeover, they looked weak and confused. The people of Russia simply did not take them seriously as leaders.

Then there was the swaggering figure of Boris Yeltsin. At this moment of crisis for Russia, he stood firmly on the side of Gorbachev's **liberal** reforms. When the Soviet parliament building was under threat from the plotters, he climbed on top of a tank and rallied support against them. His bravery and defiant words made him an instant hero for ordinary people.

▲ *Yeltsin becomes the hero of the Soviet people by refusing to surrender the parliament building to the coup leaders. His defiance rallied public support against the coup.*

A different country

Gorbachev, on the other hand, never regained his power. When he arrived at Moscow airport on August 22, he announced that he was "a different person returning to a different country." But he did not realize just how much the country had changed in a few days. Thousands of Moscow citizens demonstrated outside the headquarters of the hated KGB, and then marched to the **Central Committee** building.

In spite of all his astonishing achievements, Gorbachev was now out of touch with what people wanted. He could not accept that the Communist era was over—even when it was shown that the coup leaders had all been senior Communists. His appearance in the Soviet parliament was humiliating. Members jeered him, and Yeltsin forced him to read out the names of the plotters. The following day he resigned as leader of the Soviet Communist Party.

Bit by bit, Gorbachev's world was crumbling around him. He closed down the party's Central Committee, spelling the end of **Communist** power in Russia. In November, Yeltsin banned the Communist Party altogether. Gorbachev now had no power left, and on December 25, 1991, he resigned as president.

Within 24 hours, he and Raisa had to find a new home. All he could do after this was watch from the sidelines as his country completed the revolution he had begun. At midnight on December 31, 1991, the **Soviet Union** was officially disbanded, and the label *Soviet Union* was wiped from the world map. **Russia** was now officially the **Russian Federation,** and countries such as Ukraine and Estonia became independent.

▼ *This map shows Eastern Europe and the breakaway republics. East Germany and West Germany reunited in October 1990. Czechoslovakia later broke into two countries—the Czech Republic and Slovakia.*

◀ *Gorbachev, accompanied by his wife Raisa, signs copies of his 1996 memoir in a London department store.*

Finding a new role

Gorbachev had spent his adult life working, fighting, and plotting his way up the political ladder. He found it hard to be an outsider with little influence on events in Russia. But there was still plenty for him to do. Early in 1992, he set up the Gorbachev Foundation in Moscow. Its purpose was to provide a forum (meeting place) for discussing and studying the country's politics, society, and economics. He toured both North and South America, making speeches and giving interviews. He also traveled the world as the president of Green Cross International. It is an independent organization dedicated to improving awareness of the threats to the environment.

Much of Gorbachev's time was taken up with writing his **memoir.** He was eager to tell his side of the story and justify his actions as leader of the Soviet Union. The book was published in Russia in 1995 and in a number of foreign translations the following year. It was a huge success, especially abroad. This encouraged him to make one last effort to regain power. He ran for president of Russia in 1996 but received less than one percent of the vote. It was the final rejection.

Gorbachev continued with his speaking tours and public projects. But fate had another cruel blow to strike. He and Raisa had always done a lot of work for charity, especially in raising money for Soviet children suffering from cancer and **leukemia.** Tragically, Raisa herself died of leukemia in September 1999.

Gorbachev's Legacy

When Mikhail Gorbachev became **general secretary** in 1985, the world was a different place. The **Cold War** between East and **West** had dominated global events for 40 years. People lived in daily fear of a nuclear conflict that could wipe out their entire civilization. The **Soviet Union** itself was a lumbering, sickly giant ruled by old men who wanted nothing to change. Gorbachev promised that he could not only reform his country, but bring lasting peace to the world. He succeeded—but not exactly in the way he wanted.

Ending the Cold War

Gorbachev surprised Western leaders. Warm, humorous, sharp, and sociable, he was the exact opposite of previous Soviet bosses. He was also willing to make compromises and was sincere in wanting to eliminate **nuclear weapons.**

FOR A MAP OF THE PLACES MENTIONED, SEE PAGE 52.

The result was astonishing progress in his **summit** meetings with U.S. presidents Reagan and Bush. Within five years, they had agreed to withdraw huge numbers of troops and weapons from Europe, and the end of the Cold War was in sight.

◀ The collapse of the Soviet Union created new problems. One of the greatest tragedies took place in the **republic** of Chechnya, which rebelled against continuing Russian control. Russian troops launched a savage and long-running campaign to crush the revolt. This is how the Chechen capital looked in February 2000, after several years of violence. The armored vehicle is manned by Russian troops.

▶ *An old woman scavenges for food in Moscow during the severe winter of 1998. The enormous political changes introduced by Gorbachev did nothing to prevent the Russian economic slump, which brought widespread poverty and hardship.*

Gorbachev again hurried the peace process along by lowering the **iron curtain.** He allowed the **Eastern bloc** countries to break free of the Soviet Union and decide their own destinies within Europe. This was probably his finest achievement.

Taking Communism apart

Gorbachev's effect on Russia was just as spectacular, but less successful. "We had to change everything," said Gorbachev in his final speech on Soviet television. However, he could hardly have known just how damaging that change would be. He believed that his policies of **glasnost** and **perestroika** would reform and improve **Communism.** He thought he could rebuild the Soviet Union by lifting state controls, introducing **democratic** elections, and encouraging free speech.

He was disastrously wrong. The reforms actually helped to destroy both the **Communist** Party and the Soviet Union. The resulting chaos swept Gorbachev himself out of power. On top of this, his policies drove the economy into even deeper trouble. Yet, even though his own plans failed, they gave Soviets the chance to change their country forever.

On Gorbachev's part in ending the Cold War:
"He may not have done so alone, but what happened would not have happened without him. That cannot be said of anyone else."

(Raymond L. Garthoff, U.S. State Department)

Timeline

1931	Born on March 2 in Privolnoye, Stavropol region
1933–1934	Famine spreads in the Stavropol region
1941	German forces invade the **Soviet Union**
1950	Enters Moscow State University
1952	Becomes full member of the Communist Party
1953	Stalin dies Gorbachev marries Raisa Titorenko
1955	Graduates from university and returns to Stavropol
1956	Appointed **first secretary** of Stavropol **Komsomol**
1957	Birth of daughter Irina
1958	Elected second secretary of local district Komsomol
1961	Elected first secretary of the same committee
1962	Appointed party organizer for the region
1963	Appointed head of department for party organization in Stavropol
1964	Khrushchev dismissed, and Brezhnev takes power
1968	Soviet troops invade Czechoslovakia
1970	Appointed party first secretary for Stavropol
1971	Elected member of **Central Committee**
1978	Appointed secretary for agriculture
1979	Elected candidate member of **Politburo** Soviet troops invade Afghanistan

1980	Becomes full member of Politburo
1982	Brezhnev dies and is succeeded by Andropov
1984	Andropov dies and is succeeded by Chernenko
1985	Chernenko dies and is succeeded by Gorbachev
	Gorbachev meets Reagan in their first **summit**
1986	Announces program of **perestroika,** or rebuilding
	Chernobyl **nuclear power plant** disaster
	First troop withdrawals from Afghanistan
	Second summit with Reagan
1987	Proposes first political reforms
	Gorbachev visits Great Britain and the United States
1988	Calls for **glasnost,** or openness
	Treaty signed to end Soviet involvement in Afghanistan
	Becomes chairman of Supreme Soviet
	Announces major reduction in Soviet armed forces
1989	Free elections for **Congress of People's Deputies**
	Estonia and Latvia declare independence
	Noncommunist government elected in Poland
	Fall of the Berlin Wall
	First summit meeting with President Bush, in Malta
1990	Travels to Lithuania, scene of growing unrest
	Free local elections in Soviet Union
	Elected president of Soviet Union
	Many **republics** declare independence
	Awarded **Nobel Prize** for peace
1991	Yeltsin elected Russian president
	Attempted **coup** against Gorbachev fails
	Gorbachev resigns
1992	Soviet Union ceases to exist
	Establishes Gorbachev Foundation in Moscow
1995	Publication of **memoir** in Russia
1996	Gorbachev fails to be elected as Russian president
1999	Raisa dies

Key People of Gorbachev's Time

Andropov, Yuri (1914–1984) Andropov became the Soviet **Communist** Party **general secretary** in 1982. People expected a hard-liner, but he surprised them by calling for world peace and the reduction of **nuclear weapons.**

Brezhnev, Leonid (1906–1982) Beginning in 1945, he was a close political ally of Khrushchev, whom he succeeded as Soviet Communist Party general secretary in 1964. During his long period in power, he allowed almost no progress, keeping tight control over Eastern Europe and building up Soviet armed forces. He was responsible for the disastrous invasion of Afghanistan in 1979.

Khrushchev, Nikita (1894–1971) As leader of Ukraine in the 1940s, he **purged** many opponents of Stalin. After Stalin's death in 1953, he was just as ruthless in getting rid of rivals, becoming chairman of the **Soviet Union** in 1958. He surprised many by his attacks on Stalinism and by his attempt to steer away from rule by terror (for example, by reducing the power of the **KGB**). Communist Party leaders forced him from office in 1964.

Reagan, Ronald (1911–) Reagan served as president of the United States from 1980 to 1988. Reagan entered politics after a successful career as a film actor. Though firmly conservative and anti-Communist, he was able to form a productive relationship with Gorbachev, which led to progress in arms reduction.

Stalin, Joseph (1879–1953) Stalin worked closely with Lenin during the **Russian Revolution** of 1917. After Lenin's death, he savagely eliminated rivals. By 1927 had became virtual **dictator,** using his **secret police** to suppress all possible opposition. In 1945, he forced or tricked other **Allied leaders** into placing Eastern Europe under his control.

Yeltsin, Boris (1931–) Yeltsin became the first **democratically** elected president of the **Russian Federation** in 1990. Gorbachev brought Yeltsin to the **Kremlin** as head of construction in 1985. He was forced to resign after his harsh criticism of Gorbachev. He returned to power as mayor of Moscow.

Soviet Government

The Soviet Union had a parliament called the Supreme Soviet, elected by the people. However, until 1989, citizens had only one choice—to vote for the candidate selected by the Communist Party. No other party was allowed to put forward candidates. The party actually controlled the country, and the job of the Supreme Soviet was simply to accept party decisions.

The Communist Party of the Soviet Union

General Secretary
(party head)

Politburo
(made policy; Soviet Union's most powerful body) 12 to 15 members

Central Committee 360 members

Communist Party Congress
(approved decisions of the Politburo)
5,000 delegates
from lower levels

Regional organizations

District organizations

Local organizations
(farms, factories, offices, etc.)

The Federal Government

Chairman
(actually the head of state)

Supreme Soviet
(wrote laws and administered them)
271 members in each of two houses

Congress of People's Deputies
(elected members of the Supreme Soviet) 2,250 members—almost all Communist

Sources for Further Research

Gorbachev, Mikhail. *Memoirs*. New York: Doubleday, 1996.

Gorbachev, Mikhail. *Conversations with Gorbachev: On Perestroika, the Prague Spring, and the Crossroads of Socialism*. New York: Columbia University Press, 2002.

Hatt, Christine. *The End of the Cold War*. Milwaukee: Gareth Stevens Incorporated, 2002.

Kelly, Nigel. *The Fall of the Berlin Wall*. Chicago: Heinemann Library, 2000.

Matthews, John R. *The Rise and Fall of the Soviet Union*. Farmington Hills, Mich.: Gale Group, 1999.

Miles, Harvey, *The Fall of the Soviet Union*. Danbury, Conn.: Scholastic Library Publishing, 2000.

McCauley, Martin. *Gorbachev*. White Plains, N.Y.: Longman Publishing Group, 2000.

Rice, Earle Jr. *The Cold War: the Collapse of Communism*. Farmington Hills, Mich.: Gale Group, 2000.

Taylor, David. *The Cold War*. Chicago: Heinemann Library, 2001.

Glossary

Allied leaders leaders of the United States, Great Britain, the Soviet Union, and other countries that fought on their side during World War II

arms race a competition between countries to have bigger, better, and more weapons of war

capitalism economic system that allows free competition and private ownership of the manufacturing and distribution of goods. Capitalism's main aim is to build up capital, or money.

Central Committee main body of the Soviet Communist Party, elected at each Party Congress and including the most important officials

Cold War period of tension that existed between capitalist and Communist countries between 1945 and 1991

collective farming system in which laborers are forced to work on state farms. By 1937 all Soviet farming was done collectively.

Communism political system, such as that in the Soviet Union, based on state ownership of manufacturing and distribution of goods, centralized planning and government by a single party. A person or party supporting Communism is described as Communist.

Congress of People's Deputies new and democratically elected parliament for the Soviet Union, first convened in 1989. Its 2,250 deputies were elected for a five-year term.

coup sudden action taken to gain power or win control of a government

delegate elected person who represents others

democracy system of government in which every citizen is allowed to vote and have a say in laws and governmental actions

dictator ruler who has complete power over government

district prosecutor lawyer who conducts the prosecution, or case against a person, in criminal trials

East Berlin capital of East Germany after World War II. When Germany was divided among the Allies after World War II, the Soviet Union took control of the eastern part of the country, the part in which Berlin lay. Berlin itself was divided into eastern and western parts. Eventually, the other Allies withdrew from the western half of Germany, but West Berlin stayed democratic. The Soviets continued to control East Germany and East Berlin. In 1961 the East German government built the Berlin Wall to keep its citizens from escaping to West Berlin.

Eastern bloc countries of Eastern Europe associated with the Soviet Union in the Warsaw Pact

first secretary top official in government or local department

general secretary top party official in the Soviet Union and thus the country's leader

glasnost openness in politics and public discussion, plus freedom of information

iron curtain imaginary, or sometimes real, barrier that divided the Communist East and the capitalist West in Europe

Islam religion based on the teachings of the Prophet Muhammad

KGB Initials for the Russian words for Committee of State Security, or state police force, responsible for controlling and gathering information

Komsomol Young Communist league, open to young people from the ages of 14 to 28

Kremlin old fortified center of Moscow, used as Soviet government headquarters

labor camp prison settlement where inmates are forced to work

leukemia disease that stops the production of normal blood cells

liberal believing in the freedom of people to act and express themselves as they choose

memoir an autobiographical account of important events in a person's life

Nazis followers of Adolf Hitler in Germany

Nobel Prize any one of six prizes awarded by the Swedish Nobel Foundation for outstanding achievements in science, literature, and world peace

nuclear power plant power station that produces electricity using the energy from the splitting of atoms

nuclear weapons bombs, missiles, and other weapons that use the destructive power of nuclear energy (the splitting of atoms)

one-party system government by a single political party, elected or otherwise

Party Congress most important Communist Party meeting, which took place every five years to review policies and elect a new Central Committee and Politburo

patron person in a position of power who gives help and support to someone who is trying to achieve something

perestroika a Russian word that means reforming or rebuilding; Gorbachev's policy to modernize the Soviet economy

Politburo Political Bureau of the Central Committee, the party's key decision-making body

political prisoner someone who is imprisoned for his or her political beliefs rather than for a crime

procurator official who acts for the state as public prosecutor in law cases

propaganda spreading of ideas and information for political purposes

purge to remove all one's opponents or possible enemies by force

radioactive dust particles contaminated with radioactivity, a dangerous form of energy that results from a nuclear reaction

Red Banner red flag that was the worldwide symbol of Communism

republic country with a constitution and no monarch. In the Soviet Union, a country that is part of a federation but that has some powers to govern itself.

resistance fighter someone who fights against the established government of a country

Russia largest of the fifteen Soviet republics, also known simply as the Russian Federation

Russian Revolution uprising of 1917 that overthrew the czar (monarch) of Russia and gave power to the Bolsheviks. They set up soviets, or elected councils, to govern the country and establish a Communist state.

secret police police force that works mostly in secret to control dissidents and ensure state security

socialism belief in a social system that is run for the good of the community and in which the means of making and selling goods are owned by everyone

sovereign state independent country that governs itself

Soviet Union Union of Soviet Socialist Republics. A huge country formed in 1922 from fifteen formerly independent countries in eastern Europe and northern Asia. The word *soviet* comes from the name given to elected councils that were set up at the time of the Russian Revolution.

stagnation condition in which there is no growth or movement

steppe vast, grass-covered plains stretching from southeastern Europe to Siberia

strategic arms weapons so powerful that they dictate the way in which countries organize their defense systems

Strategic Defense Initiative (SDI) U.S. idea to protect the country from nuclear attack with laser weapons stationed in space

strike refusing to work as a way of making a protest

summit meeting of the leaders of the most powerful nations

superpower powerful nation, often using nuclear threat to dominate other countries. During the Cold War, the term was generally applied only to the United States and Soviet Union.

trade agreement treaty between countries over the supply of goods or freedom to trade

United Nations international organization of independent countries formed in 1945 to promote international security and cooperation

Warsaw Pact organization of Eastern bloc countries founded in 1955 and pledged to help defend one another in case of attack. It was created in response to the North Atlantic Treaty Organization (NATO), established by the Western powers in 1954.

West, Western political, rather than geographical name for the industrialized countries of Western Europe, North America, Australia, and New Zealand

Index